Introd.

Welcome to the "Layoff to Lift-Off" (Reclaiming your Career Path) Workbook. This workbook is designed to be a comprehensive guide and support system for individuals who have experienced the challenge of a layoff. While a layoff can feel like a setback, it is important to recognize it as an opportunity for transformation—a chance to bounce back stronger, enhance your skills, and ultimately discover new and fulfilling employment opportunities.

Losing a job is often an unexpected turn of events that can disrupt not only your professional life but also your sense of identity and purpose. It is natural to experience a wide range of emotions during this period, including shock, disappointment, fear, and even anger. These emotions are valid and deserve acknowledgment. However, it is equally important to remember that a layoff is not a reflection of your personal worth or abilities. Instead, it can serve as a pivotal moment for growth and self-improvement. This workbook, "Layoff to Lift-Off" (Reclaiming your Career Path), is your roadmap to making the most out of this transitional phase in your career.

This project was born out of a deeply personal experience. Like many, I faced the uncertainty and emotional turmoil of a layoff. But rather than allowing this event to define me, I chose to see it as an opportunity. I embarked on a journey of self-discovery, skill enhancement, and ultimately, success. Through the steps outlined in this workbook, you too can navigate your post-layoff journey with purpose and determination, turning what may seem like a setback into a powerful comeback.

In the following pages, you will find a structured plan designed to help you regain control of your career trajectory. This plan is not just about finding a new job; it is about reclaiming your confidence, redefining your career goals, and setting yourself up for long-term success. You will be guided through each step, from maintaining a positive mindset to setting achievable goals, with practical advice and actionable strategies.

Specifically, this workbook will help you to:

- Maintain a Positive Attitude: Learn how to embrace challenges with a growth mindset and turn obstacles into opportunities.

- Establish a Daily Routine: Discover the importance of structure and how to create a routine that keeps you focused, motivated, and productive.

- Assess Your Skills and Goals: Take a deep dive into your skills, experiences, and career aspirations to craft a compelling narrative for your job search.

- Utilize AI Tools: Leverage modern technology to enhance your resume, pinpoint areas for improvement, and access relevant learning resources.

- Expand Your Professional Network: Learn effective strategies for building and utilizing your professional network to uncover job opportunities.

- Prepare for Interviews: Equip yourself with the tools and techniques to present your best self during interviews, leaving a lasting impression on potential employers.

- Set Achievable Goals: Break down your job search into manageable milestones, allowing you to track your progress and stay motivated.

Remember, recovering from a layoff takes time and effort. It is a journey that requires patience, resilience, and the willingness to embrace change. However, with dedication and the guidance provided in this workbook, you can emerge stronger and more prepared for the next phase of your career journey.

So, let's begin this transformative journey together. "Layoff to Lift-Off" (Reclaiming your Career Path) is more than just a guide—it is your companion in this journey towards reclaiming your career, rebuilding your confidence, and realizing your full potential. Your success story starts here.

Step 1: Embrace the Situation

Losing your job, no matter the circumstances, can be one of the most challenging and emotional experiences in your professional life. It can feel like the ground has been pulled out from under you, leaving you with feelings of uncertainty, fear, and even anger. However, the first step in "Layoff to Lift-Off" (Reclaiming your Career Path) is to embrace the situation and approach it with a positive, proactive mindset. This step is crucial because it lays the foundation for everything that follows. How you choose to perceive and respond to this situation will significantly impact your ability to navigate it successfully.

Key Points to Remember

1. **It's Not Personal:** It's important to understand that a layoff is not a reflection of your personal worth or abilities. In many cases, layoffs are the result of business decisions, economic factors, or industry changes that are beyond your control. You are not alone in facing this challenge; it can happen to anyone, regardless of their skills or job performance. Recognizing this helps to remove the burden of self-blame and allows you to focus on what lies ahead.

2. **Your Value Extends Beyond Your Job:** While your job may have been a significant part of your life, it doesn't define your entire identity. You have a unique set of skills, experiences, and qualities that make you valuable, both professionally and personally. This is an opportunity to rediscover those aspects of yourself that may have been overshadowed by your job role. Use this time to reconnect with your passions, strengths, and aspirations.

3. **Focus on the Future:** Dwelling on the past or feeling resentful won't change the circumstances. Instead, shift your focus to the opportunities that lie ahead. This is a chance for personal and professional growth, and it can lead to a better future. Every setback is a setup for a comeback—this is your moment to redefine your career path and set new, ambitious goals for yourself.

Action Steps

- **Reflect on Your Initial Reaction:** Take a moment to reflect on your initial reaction to being laid off. Acknowledge any negative emotions you may have experienced, such as anger, sadness, or fear. It's important to process these emotions rather than suppress them. Write down your thoughts and feelings in a journal to help you gain clarity and perspective.

- **Acknowledge You Are Not Alone:** Remind yourself that you are not alone in this experience. Many successful individuals have faced layoffs and have used them as a stepping stone to greater achievements. Research stories of well-known figures who have gone through similar experiences. Understanding that others have walked this path before you—and have come out stronger on the other side—can be incredibly reassuring.

- **Use This Period for Growth:** Consider how you can use this transition period as an opportunity for self-improvement and growth. What skills do you want to develop? What career goals do you want to pursue? This is your chance to pivot, explore new interests, or even pursue a completely different career path if that's where your passion lies. Make a list of potential skills or areas you would like to explore, and start setting some preliminary goals.

- **Create a Positive Affirmation:** Write down a positive affirmation or mantra that you can refer to when you need encouragement during your job search journey. For example, "I am resilient, capable, and determined to succeed," or "Every challenge is an opportunity for growth." Place this affirmation somewhere visible—on your bathroom mirror, your computer screen, or your phone—so you can see it daily and remind yourself of your strength and potential.

Embracing the situation is the first and most critical step in turning a layoff into a transformative experience. It sets the tone for the rest of your journey in "Layoff to Lift-Off" (Reclaiming your Career Path). By accepting what has happened and choosing to move forward with a positive, growth-oriented mindset, you empower yourself to take control of your future. Stay positive, stay motivated, and keep your eyes on the horizon—your next opportunity is waiting for you.

Step 2: Daily Routine

A structured daily routine can be a lifeline during the challenging period following a layoff. It provides much-needed stability and a sense of purpose, helping you to navigate each day with intention and focus. Developing and adhering to a routine can significantly enhance your productivity, boost your morale, and ensure that you remain on track as you pursue your career goals. In the context of "Layoff to Lift-Off" (Reclaiming your Career Path), your daily routine is more than just a schedule—it is the foundation upon which your journey toward a brighter future is built.

Why a Daily Routine Matters

When you are no longer bound by the structure of a regular workday, it can be tempting to let time slip away, leading to feelings of aimlessness and frustration. A well-structured routine combats this by creating a sense of normalcy and control, both of which are crucial during periods of transition. Psychologically, routines help reduce stress and anxiety by providing predictability and order. They enable you to set clear priorities, stay motivated, and measure progress—essential factors for success in your job search and personal development.

Establishing a routine also serves as a powerful psychological anchor, giving you something to rely on amidst the uncertainty of a job search. It can transform your mindset from one of passivity and helplessness to one of proactive engagement and empowerment. With a routine, you can take deliberate steps each day toward your goals, ensuring that you are making the most of your time and energy.

Key Components of Your Daily Routine

1. **Set a Consistent Start Time:**

- o **The Importance of Consistency:** One of the most important aspects of a daily routine is setting a consistent start time. This not only helps regulate your body's internal clock, making it easier to wake up and go to sleep at regular hours, but it also sets the tone for a productive day. When you start your day at the same time each morning, you create a rhythm that helps you transition smoothly into your daily tasks.

- o **How to Implement It:** Choose a time to begin your day and stick to it, even on weekends. For instance, if you decide to start your day at 7:30 AM, set your alarm for the same time every day. This consistency will help you build momentum and reduce the temptation to stay in bed or procrastinate.

2. **Morning Activity:**

- o **The Power of a Positive Start:** How you begin your day can significantly impact your mood and productivity. Engaging in a positive, energizing activity in the morning can boost your mental and physical well-being, setting a positive tone for the rest of the day. Morning activities like a brisk walk, exercise, meditation, or even journaling can invigorate your body and mind, making you more focused and ready to tackle the day's challenges.

- o **Selecting the Right Activity:** Choose a morning activity that resonates with you and leaves you feeling refreshed and motivated. For example, you might opt for a 30-minute jog in your neighborhood, a yoga session, or reading an inspiring book or article. The key is to select an activity that you genuinely enjoy and that helps you start the day with a sense of accomplishment.

3. **Focused Work Periods:**

   o **Structuring Your Day for Success:** Once you have started your day on a positive note, it's essential to dedicate specific blocks of time to job searching, learning, and updating your resume. This is where your routine becomes a powerful tool for managing your time effectively. By creating focused work periods, you can ensure that you are making steady progress toward your goals without becoming overwhelmed.

   o **Implementing Focused Work Periods:** Break your day into segments, each dedicated to a specific task. For example, you might allocate the first two hours of your workday to job searching, the next hour to learning a new skill or completing an online course, and another hour to updating your resume or networking online. Use tools like timers or apps to help you stay on task and prevent distractions during these periods.

4. **Self-Care:**

   o **The Importance of Self-Care:** In the midst of a job search, it can be easy to neglect self-care, but maintaining your physical and mental well-being is crucial. Self-care is not a luxury; it's a necessity that helps you stay balanced, reduce stress, and maintain a positive outlook. Whether it's engaging in a hobby, spending time with loved ones, or practicing mindfulness, self-care should be an integral part of your daily routine.

- ○ **Incorporating Self-Care into Your Routine:** Allocate specific times in your day for self-care activities. This could be as simple as taking a walk in the afternoon, enjoying a relaxing bath, or setting aside time to read a good book. Remember, taking care of yourself is essential for staying energized and focused during your job search. By making self-care a priority, you'll be better equipped to handle the challenges that come your way.

Creating Your Daily Schedule

Now that you understand the key components of a productive daily routine, it's time to put them into action by creating your own schedule. Here's how you can structure your day:

- **Morning (7:30 AM - 8:00 AM):** Wake up and engage in your chosen morning activity, such as a walk or meditation. This sets a positive tone for the day and prepares you mentally and physically for the tasks ahead.

- **Mid-Morning (8:00 AM - 10:00 AM):** Focus on job searching. Use this time to browse job boards, update your LinkedIn profile, and submit applications. This is your prime time for productivity, so make sure to eliminate distractions.

- **Late Morning (10:00 AM - 11:00 AM):** Learning and skill development. Enroll in an online course or watch tutorials that will help you acquire new skills relevant to your career goals. Continuous learning keeps you competitive and motivated.

- **Midday (11:00 AM - 12:00 PM):** Resume updates and networking. Use this time to refine your resume and reach out to your professional network. Networking can open doors to opportunities you might not find through traditional job searches.

- **Lunch Break (12:00 PM - 1:00 PM):** Take a break to enjoy a healthy meal and recharge. Step away from your computer and engage in a relaxing activity.

- **Afternoon (1:00 PM - 3:00 PM):** Continue with focused work periods, whether it's more job searching, learning, or completing any remaining tasks from the morning. Stay disciplined and avoid distractions.

- **Late Afternoon (3:00 PM - 4:00 PM):** Self-care time. Engage in activities that help you relax and de-stress, such as a hobby, a short nap, or spending time with family or friends.

- **Evening (4:00 PM - 5:00 PM):** Review your day's progress and set goals for the next day. Reflect on what went well and what could be improved. End your workday on a positive note.

Action Steps

- **Choose a Consistent Start Time:** Decide on a time to begin your day and stick to it. Whether you're an early bird or a night owl, consistency is key to establishing a routine that works for you.

- **Identify a Morning Activity:** Select a morning activity that energizes you and sets a positive tone for the day.

This could be a 30-minute walk, yoga, or reading an inspiring book. Make it a non-negotiable part of your routine.

- **Plan Your Work Periods:** Allocate dedicated time for job searching, learning, and updating your resume. Be realistic about how much time you can commit each day, and use tools like calendars or apps to stay organized.

- **Schedule Breaks and Self-Care:** Ensure that your routine includes time for self-care. This could be enjoying a favorite hobby, spending time with loved ones, or practicing mindfulness exercises. Self-care is essential for maintaining a healthy mindset.

- **Create a Daily Schedule:** Use a calendar or planner to keep track of your tasks and appointments. Having a visual representation of your day can help you stay on track and ensure that you're making the most of your time.

Staying Committed

Remember, your daily routine is a powerful tool for maintaining a sense of purpose and productivity during your job search. It's not just about filling your day with activities—it's about creating a structure that supports your goals and well-being. Embrace your routine as a valuable part of your "Layoff to Lift-Off" (Reclaiming your Career Path) journey. Stay committed, and you'll steadily make progress toward your goals. Even on days when motivation wanes, your routine will keep you grounded and moving forward.

Consistency is key. While it may take time to adjust to a new routine, the effort you put into maintaining it will pay off in the long run. Each day that you stick to your routine brings you one step closer to your career goals, and to reclaiming the path that is uniquely yours.

Day 1: Assess Your Skills and Goals

The first day of your "Layoff to Lift-Off" journey is all about setting a strong foundation. This day is designed to help you transition from the shock of a layoff to proactive steps that will pave the way for your next career opportunity. By the end of Day One, you'll have a clear understanding of where you stand, what you need to improve, and how to start moving forward with purpose and confidence.

Step 3: Morning Routine (Continued)

Consistency and Purpose Maintaining your morning routine is crucial for establishing consistency in your daily life. On the first day of your journey, this routine becomes even more significant. It sets a positive tone for the day, signaling to your mind and body that you are in control and ready to take action. Whether it's a morning jog, meditation, or reading a motivational book, starting your day with an activity that energizes and centers you will help you approach the tasks ahead with a clear mind and a positive attitude.

Building Momentum The key to a successful morning routine is consistency. As you move through the coming days, this routine will help you build momentum. Each morning that you wake up and engage in your chosen activity, you're not only reinforcing a positive habit but also reminding yourself of your commitment to this journey. This momentum will carry you through challenges and help you maintain focus, even on difficult days.

Step 4: Review Your Current Resume and Job Description

Taking Stock of Where You Are Now that you've set a positive tone for the day, it's time to dive into the practical aspects of your job search. Start by pulling out your current resume and a job description for your most recent role. Reviewing these documents is an essential first step in understanding how well your resume reflects your actual job experience and whether it aligns with industry expectations.

Aligning Your Resume with Reality Begin by carefully reading through your job description. Pay attention to the specific tasks and responsibilities outlined in the document. Then, compare this with the corresponding sections in your resume. Are all the key responsibilities and achievements from your job description accurately reflected in your resume? Have you included all relevant accomplishments, or are there important aspects missing?

Identifying Gaps and Opportunities As you compare your resume with the job description, note any discrepancies or gaps. Perhaps you've omitted certain responsibilities, or maybe your resume doesn't fully capture the scope of your achievements. Identifying these gaps is the first step in creating a more accurate and compelling resume. This process also helps you recognize areas where you might need to gain additional skills or experience to meet the expectations for similar roles in the future.

Step 5: Reflect on Your Job Responsibilities

Understanding Your Role Next, take some time to reflect on your day-to-day activities in your previous job. Think about the tasks you handled, the challenges you faced, and the successes you achieved. This reflection is not just about listing duties—it's about understanding the impact you made in your role and how your contributions added value to the company.

Quantifying Your Achievements One of the most powerful ways to enhance your resume is by quantifying your accomplishments. Think about how you can express the impact of your work in measurable terms. Did you increase sales, reduce costs, or improve efficiency? Quantifying your achievements with metrics like percentages, dollar amounts, or time saved makes your resume more compelling and gives potential employers a clearer picture of your value.

Emotional Context and Professional Growth Reflecting on your job responsibilities also involves considering the emotional and professional growth you experienced in your role. What were the moments that challenged you the most, and how did you overcome them? How did these experiences shape you as a professional? Including this emotional context in your resume (where appropriate) or in your cover letter can help convey your personal growth and resilience.

Step 6: Explore Higher Progression Roles

Aiming Higher Now that you've reviewed your current role, it's time to look ahead and explore higher-level roles that you're interested in. Even if you're not currently qualified for these roles, identifying them now can help you understand the skills and experience you need to acquire to reach your career goals. This step is about setting your sights on the future and envisioning where you want your career to go.

Researching Job Descriptions Find job descriptions for the higher progression roles you're interested in. Pay close attention to the qualifications, skills, and experience required. Comparing these with your current resume will help you identify the gaps in your experience and the areas where you need to improve. This research will also give you insight into industry trends and the skills that are becoming increasingly important in your field.

Setting Goals for Growth Once you've identified the gaps between your current qualifications and the requirements for these higher-level roles, start setting goals for growth. Whether it's learning a new software program, gaining leadership experience, or developing a specific technical skill, setting clear, actionable goals will help you work toward these roles systematically.

Step 7: Seek AI Guidance

Leveraging AI for Personalized Advice In today's digital age, AI tools can be incredibly valuable for job seekers. Use an AI program, such as Chat GPT or another AI source, to simulate a conversation with a virtual "VP of Operations" or a relevant title in your field. This simulation can provide you with personalized advice, insights, and even potential interview questions based on the job descriptions you've reviewed.

Simulating Real-World Scenarios One of the benefits of using AI is that it allows you to simulate real-world scenarios without the pressure of an actual interview. You can practice answering questions, receive feedback on your responses, and even explore how your resume might be perceived by a hiring manager. This kind of preparation can boost your confidence and help you refine your approach.

Identifying Areas for Improvement AI tools can also help you identify weaknesses or areas for improvement in your resume or job search strategy. By inputting your resume and job descriptions into the AI, you can receive suggestions on how to better align your resume with the roles you're targeting. This feedback can be invaluable as you work to strengthen your application materials.

Step 8: Evaluate Your Resume

Objective Evaluation With the feedback from the AI tool, take a closer look at your resume. Consider the AI's suggestions and evaluate how well your resume aligns with the job descriptions you're targeting. This step is about being objective and critical— don't be afraid to make significant changes if necessary.

Strengthening Your Resume Based on the AI's evaluation, start making adjustments to your resume. This might involve adding new sections, rephrasing bullet points, or including more specific achievements. The goal is to ensure that your resume not only reflects your current experience but also positions you as a strong candidate for the roles you're pursuing.

Ensuring Accuracy and Honesty As you make changes, be sure to maintain accuracy and honesty in your resume. It's important to present yourself in the best possible light, but any embellishments or inaccuracies can backfire during the interview process. Keep your resume truthful, and let your genuine skills and experiences shine through.

Step 9: Compare Job Descriptions

Identifying Commonalities and Differences Next, compare the job description for your most recent role with the job description for the higher-level role you're targeting. What are the common skills and experiences required for both positions? What are the key differences? This comparison will help you understand what's expected as you move up in your career and how you can position yourself to meet these expectations.

Gap Analysis As you compare the two job descriptions, conduct a gap analysis to identify any areas where your experience or skills might be lacking. This analysis is a crucial step in understanding what you need to work on to qualify for higher-level roles. It also helps you prioritize which skills or experiences to focus on in your job search and professional development.

Strategizing for Career Growth Use the insights from your gap analysis to develop a strategy for career growth. This might involve seeking out specific projects, volunteering for leadership roles, or enrolling in courses that will help you build the skills you need. Having a clear strategy will make your job search more targeted and effective.

Step 10: Request Learning Resources

Utilizing Online Resources After identifying the gaps in your resume, ask the AI tool to recommend learning resources such as YouTube videos, LinkedIn Learning courses, or other online educational materials. These resources can help you quickly acquire the skills and knowledge needed to close those gaps and strengthen your qualifications.

Building a Learning Plan Based on the resources provided by the AI, create a learning plan that outlines the courses or videos you'll complete over the next few weeks. Make sure to include specific goals for each resource, such as mastering a particular software program or developing a new technical skill. A structured learning plan will help you stay focused and ensure that you're making consistent progress.

Staying Current with Industry Trends In addition to filling gaps in your resume, use this opportunity to stay current with industry trends. The job market is constantly evolving, and keeping your skills up to date will make you a more competitive candidate. Continuously seek out new learning opportunities to ensure that you're staying ahead of the curve.

Step 11: Enhance Software Skills

Identifying Key Software Skills As you review job descriptions for higher-level roles, you may notice that certain software skills are frequently mentioned. These skills are often essential for success in those roles, so it's important to familiarize yourself with them. Ask the AI for recommendations on which software skills would make you better qualified for the positions you're targeting.

Finding the Right Training Materials Once you've identified the key software skills you need to develop, ask the AI to recommend relevant YouTube tutorials or LinkedIn Learning courses. These resources can provide step-by-step guidance and practical exercises to help you build proficiency quickly.

Practicing and Applying Your Skills After completing the recommended training, make sure to practice your new skills regularly. Consider taking on small projects or freelance work that allows you to apply what you've learned in a real-world setting. The more you practice, the more confident you'll become, and the stronger your resume will be.

Step 12: Rewrite Your Resume

Aligning with Job Descriptions With all the insights and feedback you've gathered, it's time to rewrite your resume. Focus on aligning your resume with the job descriptions you've reviewed, highlighting the skills and experiences that are most relevant to the roles you're targeting. Make sure your resume tells a clear and compelling story about your qualifications and career trajectory.

Incorporating Impact and Emotion As you rewrite your resume, don't forget to incorporate the impact numbers and emotional context you reflected on earlier. Quantifying your achievements and adding a personal touch can make your resume stand out to potential employers. Be sure to emphasize how your contributions have made a difference in your previous roles.

Ensuring Accuracy and Formatting Before finalizing your resume, carefully review it for accuracy and formatting. Check for any typos or inconsistencies, and make sure the layout is clean and easy to read. A well-formatted resume not only looks professional but also makes it easier for hiring managers to quickly find the information they need.

Step 13: Job Applications

Applying with Confidence With your updated resume in hand, you're now ready to start applying for job opportunities. Focus on companies that align with your goals and values, and be sure to tailor your resume and cover letter for each application. This personalized approach will increase your chances of standing out and securing interviews.

Targeting the Right Companies Choose 5 to 10 companies that are a good fit for your career aspirations and start applying. Make sure to research each company thoroughly, understanding their mission, culture, and the specific role you're applying for. This knowledge will help you craft compelling applications that resonate with the hiring managers.

Tracking Your Applications Keep track of the jobs you've applied for using a spreadsheet or job search app. Include details such as the date of application, the company's name, the role, and any follow-up actions you need to take. Staying organized will help you manage your job search more effectively and ensure that you're following up on potential opportunities.

Step 14: Reflect and Rest

Acknowledging Your Efforts By the end of Day One, you may feel mentally drained from all the activities you've completed. It's important to take some time to reflect on what you've accomplished and give yourself credit for the hard work you've put in. Acknowledging your efforts is key to maintaining motivation and momentum throughout your job search journey.

Taking Time to Recharge After a productive day, it's essential to rest and recharge. Engage in an activity that relaxes and rejuvenates you, whether it's watching a movie, spending time with family, or simply taking a walk. Taking care of your mental and physical well-being is crucial for sustaining long-term productivity and success.

Looking Ahead As you wind down for the day, take a moment to look ahead to tomorrow. Consider what you've learned today and how you can apply it moving forward. Day One sets the foundation for your "Layoff to Lift-Off" journey, and by staying committed to the process, you'll continue to build on this strong start in the days to come.

Conclusion

Day One is about laying the groundwork for your job search and career advancement. By reviewing your resume, reflecting on your past experiences, and setting goals for the future, you're taking significant steps toward increasing your marketability and finding the right job opportunity. Stay committed to the process, and remember that the efforts you put in today will pay off in the days to come.

Day 2: Networking and Job Search

On Day Two of your "Layoff to Lift-Off" journey, the focus shifts towards actively expanding your network, intensifying your job search efforts, and continuing your skill development. Networking and job searching are dynamic processes that require both consistency and strategy. By dedicating time each day to these activities, you increase your chances of finding new opportunities that align with your career goals. Today's efforts will help you build the momentum needed to navigate this transitional phase with confidence and purpose.

Step 15: Morning Routine (Continued)

Reinforcing Positive Habits As you begin Day Two, start with your established morning routine, including your chosen morning activity. Whether it's a morning jog, meditation, or reading, this routine is vital in maintaining a positive and productive mindset. The consistency of a morning routine not only sets the tone for the day but also reinforces positive habits that contribute to your overall well-being.

Establishing Control and Focus A consistent morning routine provides structure, helping you feel more in control of your day. This sense of control is especially important during times of uncertainty, like a job search. By starting your day with intention and focus, you set yourself up for a productive day, ready to tackle the challenges ahead. The energy and clarity gained from a solid morning routine will be crucial as you delve into the day's networking and job search activities.

Step 16: LinkedIn Networking (Continued)

Expanding Your Network Networking is a powerful tool in any job search, and LinkedIn is one of the most effective platforms for building and maintaining professional connections. On Day Two, continue your efforts on LinkedIn by reviewing connection requests and accepting any that have been approved. Each new connection is a potential gateway to job opportunities, industry insights, and professional growth.

Building Meaningful Relationships Networking isn't just about increasing your number of connections; it's about building meaningful relationships. When someone accepts your connection request, consider sending them a thank-you message to express your appreciation for connecting. A simple message, such as, "Thank you for connecting. I look forward to engaging with your content and learning from your insights," can go a long way in establishing a positive relationship. This step personalizes your networking efforts and makes you more memorable to your connections.

Engaging with Your Network Beyond sending connection requests, actively engage with your network by liking, commenting on, or sharing relevant posts. Engaging with content not only increases your visibility on the platform but also helps you stay informed about industry trends and news. Take the time to contribute to discussions, share valuable articles, or even post your own insights. This level of engagement showcases your expertise and keeps you top-of-mind for potential job opportunities.

Step 17: Job Search (Continued)

Focused Job Searching The job search process is often time-consuming and can be mentally exhausting, but consistency is key. Dedicate 3 to 4 hours to focused job searching, just as you did on Day One. Use a combination of job search engines, company websites, and networking connections to find relevant opportunities. Keep your job search targeted and strategic, focusing on roles that align with your skills and career goals.

Utilizing Multiple Platforms Diversify your job search efforts by utilizing multiple platforms. In addition to popular job boards like Indeed, Glassdoor, and LinkedIn, explore niche job boards that cater to your industry or specific roles. Company websites are also valuable resources, as many organizations post job openings directly on their career pages before listing them on public job boards. Be thorough in your search, and don't hesitate to reach out directly to companies that interest you, even if they don't have current job openings listed.

Tracking Your Applications To manage your job search effectively, keep a detailed record of the jobs you've applied for. Create a spreadsheet or use a job search management tool to track key details, such as the job title, company name, application date, and follow-up actions. This practice helps you stay organized, prevents duplicate applications, and ensures timely follow-ups. Regularly reviewing your application history also allows you to refine your search strategy based on the responses you receive.

Step 18: Learning and Skill Development (Continued)

Commitment to Continuous Learning In today's competitive job market, continuous learning is essential for staying relevant and enhancing your employability. Continue watching the YouTube and LinkedIn Learning videos and courses recommended by the AI chatbot. Dedicate time each day to learning, whether it's acquiring new technical skills, improving your soft skills, or deepening your knowledge in a specific area. The skills you develop during this time will make you a more attractive candidate and increase your confidence during interviews.

Applying What You Learn As you progress through your courses, think about how the skills you're acquiring relate to your job goals. For instance, if you're learning a new software program, consider how it can be applied in the roles you're targeting. If you're improving your communication skills, think about how you can demonstrate these abilities in your resume, cover letter, and interviews. Applying what you learn in practical ways not only reinforces your knowledge but also enhances your resume and overall job search strategy.

Expanding Your Skillset While it's important to focus on skills that are directly related to your field, consider expanding your skillset to include complementary skills as well. For example, if you're in marketing, learning about data analysis or SEO can make you a more versatile candidate. If you're in management, improving your project management or financial analysis skills can open up new opportunities. Broadening your skillset increases your adaptability and makes you more competitive in the job market.

Step 19: Resume Updates (Continued)

Reflecting on Your Progress As you complete courses or videos, take the time to reflect on how your newly acquired skills relate to your job goals. This reflection helps you identify the most relevant skills and experiences to highlight in your resume. It's important to keep your resume current, ensuring that it accurately reflects your latest achievements and qualifications.

Showcasing New Skills When updating your resume, focus on showcasing the new skills and knowledge you've gained. Include specific examples of how you've applied these skills in practical scenarios, whether through previous work experience, volunteer projects, or personal initiatives. Emphasize how these skills can add value to potential employers, making your resume stand out in the application process.

Optimizing for ATS As you update your resume, keep in mind that many companies use Applicant Tracking Systems (ATS) to screen resumes. To increase the chances of your resume passing through these systems, ensure that it includes relevant keywords from the job descriptions you're targeting. Use clear, concise language and a simple format to make your resume ATS-friendly. An optimized resume not only improves your chances of being noticed by hiring managers but also demonstrates your attention to detail.

Step 20: Weekend Strategy (Continued)

Balancing Work and Personal Time As you approach the weekend, it's important to plan a strategy that balances your job search efforts with personal time. While it's tempting to take a break from job searching entirely, allocating specific time slots on the weekend for job-related activities can help you stay on track without feeling overwhelmed. Consider dedicating an hour or two each day to job searching, networking, or skill development, while reserving the rest of the time for relaxation and rejuvenation.

Setting Weekend Goals Setting specific goals for the weekend can help you maintain momentum in your job search. For example, you might set a goal to apply for a certain number of jobs, complete a course, or reach out to new connections on LinkedIn. These small goals keep you engaged and ensure that you're making consistent progress, even outside of the traditional workweek.

The Importance of Rejuvenation While it's important to stay productive, the weekend also offers a valuable opportunity to recharge. Use this time to engage in activities that bring you joy and relaxation, whether it's spending time with family, pursuing a hobby, or enjoying the outdoors. Taking care of your mental and physical well-being is crucial for sustaining long-term productivity and preventing burnout. A well-balanced weekend strategy leaves you refreshed and ready to tackle the challenges of the upcoming week.

Step 21: Reflection and Relaxation (Continued)

Reflecting on Your Progress At the end of Day Two, take some time to reflect on the activities you've completed and the progress you've made in your job search journey. Consider how your networking efforts have expanded your professional connections, how your job search strategy is evolving, and how your learning and skill development are enhancing your qualifications. Reflection is a powerful tool for recognizing your achievements, identifying areas for improvement, and setting intentions for the days ahead.

Engaging in Relaxation After a productive day, it's important to unwind and relax. Engaging in a hobby, spending quality time with loved ones, or simply taking a moment to enjoy a quiet evening can help you decompress and recharge. Relaxation is not just a reward for hard work—it's an essential component of a healthy and balanced job search strategy. By taking time to relax, you allow yourself to maintain energy and focus, ensuring that you're at your best when pursuing new opportunities.

Preparing for Tomorrow As you prepare for the next day, think about what you've learned from Day Two and how you can build on it. Whether it's deepening your engagement with your network, refining your job search approach, or continuing your skill development, each day brings new opportunities for growth and progress. Stay committed to your daily routine, embrace the challenges ahead, and remember that each step you take brings you closer to your career goals.

Conclusion

Day Two reinforces the importance of networking, consistent job searching, and continuous learning in your journey to recover and excel after a layoff. By dedicating time to expanding your professional connections, intensifying your job search efforts, and enhancing your skills, you are building a solid foundation for success. Stay dedicated to your daily routine, embrace each opportunity for growth, and keep your focus on the long-term goal of reclaiming your career path. Your efforts on Day Two will bring you closer to discovering new opportunities and achieving your career aspirations.

Day Three of your "Layoff to Lift-Off" journey is about solidifying the habits you've started to build and setting clear, actionable goals for your job search. It's also about preparing for the challenges ahead, including interviews and the patience required for a successful job search. By the end of today, you'll have a stronger sense of direction and the tools you need to stay motivated and persistent throughout your journey.

Step 22: Morning Routine (Continued)

Reinforcing Positive Habits As you continue with your established morning routine, it's important to recognize the power of consistency in maintaining focus and motivation. Your morning routine is more than just a series of tasks; it's a deliberate practice that sets the tone for your entire day. Whether your routine involves exercise, meditation, or reading, these activities are vital in creating a mindset that is resilient, focused, and ready to tackle the day's challenges.

The Psychological Benefits of a Morning Routine Research shows that a consistent morning routine can significantly reduce stress and increase productivity. When you begin each day with a structured routine, you minimize decision fatigue, allowing your mind to focus on more important tasks. This structure helps you start your day with a sense of accomplishment, boosting your confidence and setting a positive trajectory for the rest of your day.

Adapting and Evolving Your Routine While consistency is key, it's also important to adapt your morning routine as needed. As you progress in your job search, you may find that certain activities become more or less beneficial. Be open to adjusting your routine to better suit your evolving needs. For example, if you find that your initial activity no longer energizes you, try incorporating a new element, such as a different form of exercise or a new inspirational podcast.

Step 23: Setting Goals

The Importance of Goal Setting Goal setting is a critical step in your job search journey. It provides direction, motivation, and a clear framework for measuring progress. By setting specific and achievable goals, you break down the overwhelming process of job searching into manageable tasks. This not only makes the journey less daunting but also allows you to track your progress and celebrate small wins along the way.

SMART Goals: Specific, Measurable, Achievable, Relevant, Time-bound When setting goals, use the SMART criteria to ensure they are effective:

- **Specific:** Clearly define what you want to achieve. For example, instead of setting a vague goal like "network more," specify that you want to connect with two industry professionals each week.

- **Measurable:** Ensure that your goals have measurable outcomes so you can track your progress. For instance, aim for "one interview per week" or "apply to five jobs by Friday."

- **Achievable:** Set realistic goals that are within your reach given your current situation. Challenge yourself, but don't set goals so high that they become discouraging.

- **Relevant:** Your goals should align with your broader career objectives. Focus on activities that directly contribute to your job search, skill development, or personal growth.

- **Time-bound:** Assign deadlines to your goals. This creates a sense of urgency and helps you stay on track. For example, "Complete my LinkedIn profile update by the end of the day."

Examples of Job Search Goals

- **Networking Goals:** Connect with 5 new professionals in your industry each week. Attend one virtual networking event or webinar each month.

- **Job Application Goals:** Apply to at least three jobs per day. Tailor each application to the specific job description to increase your chances of securing an interview.

- **Skill Development Goals:** Complete one online course relevant to your career field every two weeks. Add any newly acquired skills to your resume as soon as they are gained.

Step 24: Daily Task Allocation

Structuring Your Day With your goals set, the next step is to allocate specific hours in your day to job searching, learning, and updating your resume. This structured approach ensures that you make consistent progress in all areas of your job search, rather than focusing too heavily on one at the expense of others.

Prioritizing Tasks Start by prioritizing your tasks based on importance and urgency. For instance, if you've identified networking as a crucial goal, dedicate the first part of your day to reaching out to contacts or attending networking events. If skill development is a priority, allocate uninterrupted time in the afternoon to complete online courses or tutorials.

Using Tools to Stay Organized Consider using productivity tools like to-do lists, calendars, or apps like Trello or Asana to manage your tasks. These tools help you visualize your daily schedule and ensure that you're staying on track. Set reminders for important deadlines and create checklists to mark off completed tasks. This not only keeps you organized but also gives you a sense of accomplishment as you see tasks being completed.

Balancing Job Searching and Learning It's important to strike a balance between job searching and skill development. While applying for jobs is crucial, improving your skills makes you a more competitive candidate. Allocate time in your schedule to both, ensuring that you're not neglecting one in favor of the other. For example, you might spend the morning on job applications and the afternoon on learning new skills.

Step 25: Prepare for Interviews

Proactive Interview Preparation Even before you land an interview, it's important to start preparing. Interviews can be daunting, but with the right preparation, you can approach them with confidence. Start by comparing your resume with job descriptions to identify potential weaknesses. Use AI tools to help you analyze your resume and the job descriptions. This analysis will highlight areas where you might need to improve or emphasize certain skills.

Generating Interview Questions Once you have a clear understanding of the job requirements, use AI to generate potential interview questions. These questions should be tailored to the specific job description, focusing on the skills and experiences that are most relevant. Prepare answers for these questions, drawing on your past experiences and achievements. Practice these answers until you feel confident in delivering them.

Memorizing and Adapting Answers Memorize key points for each answer but be flexible in how you deliver them. Interviews can be unpredictable, and it's important to be able to adapt your answers to different questions. Practice answering questions out loud, either in front of a mirror or with a friend, to build confidence. The more familiar you are with your responses, the more natural you'll sound during the actual interview.

Step 26: Daily Reiteration

Building a Routine of Success Repetition is key to mastering any skill, and your job search is no different. Continue repeating the daily actions you've established—job searching, learning, and updating your resume. Each day that you stick to your routine, you're building on your skills and improving your chances of landing your desired job.

Reinforcing Positive Habits By repeating these actions daily, you're reinforcing positive habits that will serve you well throughout your career. Consistency leads to mastery, and the more you engage in these activities, the more proficient and confident you'll become. Over time, what might have felt like a daunting process will become second nature, allowing you to approach each day with greater ease and confidence.

Adjusting as Needed While consistency is important, be open to adjusting your routine as needed. If you find that certain activities aren't yielding results, don't be afraid to change them. For example, if a particular job board isn't producing relevant job leads, try another one. The key is to remain flexible and adaptive, while still maintaining the core elements of your routine.

Step 27: Patience and Persistence

Understanding the Job Search Timeline It's essential to understand that finding the right job may take time. The job market is competitive, and it's normal to experience setbacks along the way. Don't be discouraged if you don't see immediate results. The most important thing is to remain patient and persistent.

Staying Motivated Maintaining a positive attitude during a job search can be challenging, especially when faced with rejections or a lack of responses. However, it's important to keep working diligently towards your goals. Remind yourself that every application submitted, every skill learned, and every connection made brings you one step closer to your desired job. Celebrate small victories along the way to stay motivated.

Overcoming Rejection Rejection is a natural part of the job search process, but it's important not to take it personally. Each rejection is an opportunity to learn and improve. Take the time to reflect on any feedback you receive and use it to strengthen your future applications and interviews. Remember that persistence is key, and every "no" brings you closer to a "yes."

Step 28: Sharing Your Job Search Status

Leveraging Your Network One of the most effective ways to find job opportunities is by sharing your job search status with your network. Let your friends, family, and professional connections know that you're actively looking for work. Don't suffer in silence; sharing your situation can lead to valuable connections and opportunities that you might not have found on your own.

Crafting Your Message When sharing your job search status, craft a clear and concise message that outlines what you're looking for. Be specific about the type of roles you're interested in and the skills you bring to the table. For example, you might say, "I'm currently seeking opportunities in digital marketing with a focus on content strategy. If you know of any openings or can introduce me to someone in this field, I would greatly appreciate it."

Following Up After sharing your job search status, be sure to follow up with any leads or connections that arise. A simple thank-you message or a quick check-in can go a long way in maintaining relationships and keeping your job search top of mind for others. Stay proactive in your networking efforts, and don't hesitate to reach out to your connections periodically to update them on your progress.

Step 29: Self-Care and Rest

Preventing Burnout Job searching can be exhausting, both mentally and physically. It's important to take time to relax, practice self-care, and recharge your energy. Burnout can hinder your job search efforts, making it difficult to stay focused and motivated. By prioritizing self-care, you ensure that you're at your best when it comes to applying for jobs, attending interviews, and networking.

Incorporating Self-Care into Your Routine Make self-care a regular part of your daily routine. This could include activities like exercise, meditation, or spending time with loved ones. Even simple acts like taking a walk, reading a book, or enjoying a hobby can help you unwind and relieve stress. The key is to find activities that rejuvenate you and help you maintain a balanced approach to your job search.

Listening to Your Body and Mind Pay attention to how you're feeling throughout your job search journey. If you start to feel overwhelmed or stressed, take a step back and give yourself permission to rest. It's okay to take breaks, and sometimes a short pause can provide the clarity and renewed energy you need to continue with your search.

Step 30: Celebrate Progress

Acknowledging Achievements As you approach the end of Day Three, take time to celebrate even the small wins you've achieved in your job search journey. Acknowledging your progress is important for maintaining motivation and boosting your confidence. Whether it's successfully completing a course, landing an interview, or making a valuable connection, each achievement deserves recognition.

Reflecting on Growth Celebrating progress also involves reflecting on how far you've come since you started your journey. Consider the skills you've developed, the knowledge you've gained, and the connections you've made. Reflecting on your growth helps you see the bigger picture and reminds you that every effort is bringing you closer to your ultimate goal.

Staying Positive and Motivated Remember that job searching is a marathon, not a sprint. By celebrating your progress, you reinforce a positive mindset that will sustain you through the ups and downs of the journey. Keep pushing forward, stay committed to your goals, and trust that your hard work will pay off in the end.

Conclusion

Day Three is about setting clear goals for your job search, staying committed to your daily routine, and preparing for future interviews. It's also a day to practice patience and persistence, understanding that the job search process requires both time and effort. By following these steps, you're setting yourself up for success and increasing your chances of finding the right opportunity. Keep pushing forward, stay positive, and remember that every step you take is bringing you closer to your career goals. Your hard work and dedication will ultimately lead to the success you're striving for.

Final Conclusion: Your Journey to Success

Congratulations! You've reached the final conclusion of the "Layoff to Lift-Off" (Reclaiming your Career Path) Workbook. This journey has been more than just a series of steps; it's been a transformative process designed to help you turn the challenge of a layoff into a powerful opportunity for personal and professional growth. As you prepare to embark on the next phase of your career, let's reflect on the key lessons and insights you've gained.

Embracing a Positive Attitude

One of the most crucial lessons you've learned is the importance of maintaining a positive attitude. From the very beginning, you recognized that a layoff, while challenging, does not define your worth. Instead, it can serve as a catalyst for new opportunities and greater achievements. By embracing this mindset, you've empowered yourself to approach each day with optimism and determination. Remember, how you perceive your situation directly influences the outcomes you achieve. A positive attitude is not just a coping mechanism—it's a strategic advantage that will continue to serve you well as you navigate future challenges.

The Power of a Structured Routine

Throughout this workbook, you've established and refined a daily routine that has become the backbone of your success. This routine provided you with discipline, focus, and a sense of purpose during a time when it would have been easy to feel lost or overwhelmed. By organizing your days with intention, you've created a structure that supports your goals and keeps you moving forward. This routine is more than just a temporary tool; it's a practice that can be carried forward into your new career, helping you maintain productivity and balance in all aspects of your life.

Skills Assessment and Continuous Improvement

A significant part of this journey involved assessing your skills, experiences, and goals. This self-assessment allowed you to identify your strengths and areas for improvement, enabling you to tailor your job search more effectively. But the process didn't stop there. You've committed to continuous learning and skill development, setting yourself apart from the competition and boosting your confidence. In a rapidly evolving job market, the ability to adapt and grow is invaluable. By making lifelong learning a core principle, you ensure that you remain competitive and capable of seizing new opportunities as they arise.

Leveraging AI and Technology

In today's digital age, leveraging AI tools like Chat GPT has become essential in optimizing your job search. You've used these tools to enhance your resume, pinpoint areas for improvement, and access valuable learning resources. This approach has not only made your job search more efficient but also more targeted and effective. As you move forward, continue to explore how technology can support your professional growth. Whether it's through AI, online courses, or networking platforms, staying tech-savvy will give you a competitive edge in the job market.

Networking: The Key to Unlocking Opportunities

Building and maintaining a professional network has been a central theme throughout this workbook. LinkedIn and other networking platforms have proven to be invaluable resources for opening doors to new opportunities. You've learned that networking is not just about collecting contacts but about building meaningful relationships. These connections can lead to job offers, partnerships, and mentorship opportunities that you might not have discovered otherwise. As you continue your career journey, make networking a regular part of your professional life. The relationships you build today will be the foundation of your success tomorrow.

Goal Setting and Achievement

Setting specific, achievable goals has kept you motivated and provided a clear sense of direction throughout your job search. By breaking down your objectives into manageable milestones, you've been able to track your progress and celebrate your achievements. Goal setting is a powerful tool that will continue to serve you well beyond this job search. As you enter your new role or pursue new ventures, regularly revisit and revise your goals to ensure you're always moving forward with purpose.

Patience, Persistence, and Resilience

The journey to finding the right job often requires patience and persistence. There may have been moments of frustration or doubt, but you've learned the value of staying resilient. This resilience is a testament to your determination and your ability to adapt in the face of adversity. As you move forward, remember that setbacks are not failures—they are opportunities to learn, grow, and come back stronger. Your persistence in the job search process has prepared you to tackle challenges in your new role with confidence and resilience.

Sharing Your Journey and Celebrating Progress

Throughout this workbook, you've been encouraged to share your job search status with your network. This openness has led to support, opportunities, and connections that have been instrumental in your journey. As you transition into the next chapter of your career, continue to share your experiences and achievements. Celebrating your progress, no matter how small, is important for maintaining motivation and building confidence. Each step forward is a testament to your hard work and dedication, and these milestones deserve recognition.

The Importance of Self-Care and Work-Life Balance

Amidst the focus on job searching and professional growth, you've also learned the importance of self-care and maintaining a healthy work-life balance. Burnout can hinder your progress, so taking time to relax, recharge, and engage in activities that bring you joy is crucial. As you step into your new career, continue to prioritize self-care. A balanced approach to work and life will not only enhance your productivity but also contribute to your overall well-being and happiness.

Looking Ahead: The Beginning of a New Chapter

As you close this workbook, it's important to recognize that this is not the end but the beginning of an exciting new chapter in your career. The tools, strategies, and mindset you've developed throughout this journey have equipped you with the resilience, adaptability, and confidence needed to navigate future challenges. The job market is filled with opportunities, and you are well-prepared to seize them.

Your success story is just around the corner. Your determination and hard work will lead you to new heights in your career. As you move forward, continue to believe in yourself and your abilities. The knowledge and experience you've gained during this journey are invaluable assets that will propel you toward success.

Final Words: Embrace the Future with Confidence

As you embark on this new chapter, go forth with confidence. You've got what it takes to recover and excel, and the opportunities that lie ahead are yours for the taking. Remember to stay true to the principles you've learned—maintain a positive attitude, continue learning and growing, and never underestimate the power of persistence.

Best of luck on your journey! Your future is bright, and the next success is within your reach.

Appendix: Notes, Progress Tracking, and Resources

In this section, you'll find space to record your thoughts and progress, as well as additional resources you may need during your *"Layoff to Lift-Off" (Reclaiming your Career Path)* journey. Feel free to use this section for personal reflections and to adjust the plan as needed.

Daily Progress Tracking:

Use the space below to track your daily progress, including tasks completed, goals met, and any challenges or successes you encountered.

Day 1:

☐ Completed Step 4: Compared Resume and Job Description.

☐ Completed Step 5: Reflected on Job Responsibilities.

☐ Completed Step 6: Identified a Higher Progression Role.

☐ Completed Step 7: Sought AI Guidance (Resume Evaluation).

☐ Completed Step 8: AI Evaluation of Resume Against Job Descriptions.

☐ Completed Step 9: Compared Job Descriptions and Identified Gaps.

☐ Completed Step 10: Requested Learning Resources.

☐ Completed Step 11: Enhanced Software Skills.

- ☐ Completed Step 12: Rewrote Resume.

- ☐ Completed Step 13: Submitted Resume to 5–10 Target Companies.

- ☐ Took Some Time to Relax and Recharge.

Day 2:

- ☐ Completed Step 15: Continued Morning Routine.

- ☐ Completed Step 16: LinkedIn Update and Networking.

- ☐ Completed Step 17: Dedicated Time for Job Search.

- ☐ Completed Step 18: Continued Learning and Skill Development.

- ☐ Completed Step 19: Updated Resume with New Skills.

- ☐ Completed Step 20: Planned Weekend Strategy for Work-Life Balance.

- ☐ Took Time for Relaxation and Self-care.

Day 3:

- ☐ Completed Step 22: Continued Morning Routine.

- ☐ Completed Step 23: Set Specific Goals.

- ☐ Completed Step 24: Allocated Daily Tasks.

- ☐ Completed Step 25: Prepared for Future Interviews.

- ☐ Completed Steps 26 and 27: Maintained Daily Routine.

- ☐ Completed Step 28: Shared Job Search Status with Network.

☐ Practiced Self-care and Took Time to Relax.

☐ Celebrated Progress Made.

Additional Notes and Resources

Use the space below to jot down any additional notes, insights, or resources you come across during your job search journey. This can include contact details of HR professionals and recruiters, specific job opportunities, or insights from networking conversations.

Note 1:

Note 2:

Note 3:

Additional Resources (List any websites, books, or articles that you find helpful):

This "Appendix" section provides you with a handy tool to track your daily progress and keep important information organized. Use it to tailor your job search journey to meet your unique needs and circumstances, and don't forget to celebrate your achievements along the way!

Notes

Made in the USA
Columbia, SC
19 November 2024

46436520R00026